CAREER BUILDING THROUGH

MUSIC, VIDEO, AND SOFTWARE MASHUPS

HOLLY CEFREY

ROSEN
PUBLISHING®

New York

To our Rosen readers, thank you for enjoying our books

Published in 2008 by The Rosen Publishing Group, Inc.
29 East 21st Street, New York, NY 10010

Library of Congress Cataloging-in-Publication Data

Cefrey, Holly.
Digital career building through music, video, and software mashups / Holly Cefrey. — 1st ed.
    p. cm. — (Digital career building)
Includes bibliographical references.
ISBN-13: 978-1-4042-1359-3 (library binding)
1. Multimedia systems—Vocational guidance—United States. 2. Music—Vocational guidance—United States. 3. Video recordings—Production and direction—Vocational guidance. I. Title.
QA76.575.C4 2008
006.7071—dc22

                                                              2007028040

Manufactured in the China

CONTENTS

CHAPTER ONE
COMBINING TECHNOLOGIES TO MAKE A BETTER PRODUCTION

The home computer has changed our existence, espe-cially as consumers. A consumer is a buyer of goods and services. As consumers, we have a wide variety of products and services from which to choose. Before the computer, we obtained these goods and services in our local shops. With the computer, we can find these things across the globe.

The computer has produced a new kind of consumer: the prosumer. This is a cross between a consumer and a producer. A producer is someone who brings various elements together to create something. Software appli-cations allow us to make our own music, videos, and various digital projects. You do not have to go to a studio

An audio engineer adjusts the sound of a track on a mixer board, or console.

for sound recording services. You can do it on your computer with software such as GarageBand or MixCraft. You do not have to go to a production studio to edit video. You can do it on your computer with software such as Final Cut Pro, Premier, and Director.

The prosumer is now also known as a professional consumer. This is a person who uses something to make other things, at a level that is semiprofessional. An audio engineer goes to school to learn about audio and sound dynamics. He or she studies sound in order to become a professional in the music and sound recording industry. He or she learns how to arrange, record, and master an audio track. A master is a final version of a recording session. He or she works in a professional or home-based studio to create a product.

The home computer user is able to master a song without relying on a solid background in sound engineering. There is a great difference, however, between a seasoned sound engineer and a newbie prosumer. A sound engineer already understands why some sounds are great together and why others seem to cancel each other out. There are many online forums where beginners and pros exchange ideas and tips, within music, film, and digital art fields.

Wearing Many Hats: The Editor, Director, and Producer

Software allows you to make your own music, videos, and digital projects. You become your own screenwriter, camera operator, director, and editor. It allows you to become the artist and production company. Software

allows you to "own" the entire creative process if you want to.

Software also allows you another feature: the ability to change other people's music, videos, and digital projects. Being able to change or modify other works has become a new art form. This art form spans across video, music, and even software applications. Projects that are made from other people's creative works are called mashups.

A mashup, also known as a mash up or mash-up, is a combination of two or more separate existing works. A part of one thing is mixed with a part from another thing to create a whole new product. Mashups are also known as bootlegs, hashups, cutups (or cut-ups), and blends.

Music Mashups

For music, a mashup is the combination of the music from one song, with the lyrics or vocal track of another song; a track is a channel on which a sound is recorded. In most studio recordings, each sound source gets its own track. The voice will have its own, and the bass, guitar, and drums will have their own. Several tracks are mixed together to make a complete work or composition. The vocal track taken from a composition is called an a cappella; this is an Italian phrase that translates as "the style of the chapel." It means without using musical instruments.

 Because mashups are a new art form, they have yet to be standardized and rated. You will come across content made for mature listeners and viewers. If you use

COMBINING TECHNOLOGIES TO
MAKE A BETTER PRODUCTION

Artists like Christina Aguilera inspire other creative works, such as mashups. Fans can pay tribute to her by combining her voice or music with other favorite artists.

video forums such as YouTube, you will find many cool mashups, without the mature content.

Editing software allows users to separate the tracks of an original recording. You can take out the singer's voice, or you can take the music out of a song so that only the desired track remains. Taking a track from a mix is also known as isolating. You pair that with the supporting track from another song. For example, you isolate Christina Aguilera's vocal track from her song "Genie in a Bottle." Next, you isolate the music from "Hard to Explain" by the Strokes. Then you remix the two tracks so they go together. Now you have a new, strangely cool song!

 The hard-driving sounds of rock and roll can be mixed with the soft vocal tracks of today's top pop performers to make exciting new music. Pictured here are the Strokes, a band from New York City.

This example was actually done in 2001 by Roy Kerr. The mix was so good that it brought global attention to the new art form. Kerr's private project also led to a new career. He was hired to do official remixes for Aguilera and other industry giants like Paul McCartney. Taking pop music and mashing it with edgier, heavier music has become known as Frankenpop, after the classic man-made creature Frankenstein.

CHECK IT OUT The song "A Stroke of Genius" (also titled "A Stroke of Genie-us") was made in 2001 by Roy Kerr, otherwise known as Freelance Hellraiser. Christina Aguilera's poppy vocal from "Genie in a Bottle" seems to change drastically when put over

Springing from the Roots of Remix

Mashup techniques are built upon the solid grounds of remixing. A remix is a different version of an original song. A simple remix can be a lengthened or extended version of your favorite song. Remixes are also samples of different songs pulled together in a long, blended track. Remixing is also used to pump up a slow song into a version you can dance to.

According to the BBC, remixing began in Jamaica during the 1960s. DJs and sound engineers wanted to test and push their sound systems to the limit. In order to do so, they needed strong beats. Instrumental versions were made of popular songs from the musical styles of ska and reggae. They were the original songs, but without the singer and some other instruments. What was left was a strong rhythm track.

Soon engineers and DJs were experimenting with the effects in their sound systems, such as adding echoes to the beats. They were speeding up or slowing the beats, or tempo. Engineers also began to lengthen the segments where instrumentals or solos occurred in the standard songs. Club-goers loved them because they could dance to their favorite songs for a bit longer.

Mashups have been popular only in the past few years. Some remixing projects are borderline mashup. The band DNA remixed musician Suzanne Vega's "Tom's Diner" with music from the group Soul II Soul in 1990. It became a global hit. A&M, Vega's record company, bought the single from DNA and released it. Is this a mashup or a great piece of remixing? Either way, mashups as we know them now stem from remixing.

the raw rock sound of the Strokes. Check out Kerr's Web site, which has more of his mashups and professional mixes: http://www.thefreelancehellraiser.com.

Disc jockeys (DJs) are now mixing many parts from many songs into one, but the traditional challenge still remains: to find a vocal that will fit over another musician's music perfectly without having to greatly edit the isolated tracks. Many DJs are adding mashups to their standard club playlists. This is because music mashups offer a fresh take on songs that have been heard many times already.

Video Mashups

Video mashups have become extremely popular in the past few years. There are video mashups based on music mashups. The new music mashup is the sound track to one or both of the original musicians' videos. An example is DJ Lobsterdust's "She Is Glamorous," which is a music video mashup of Fergie's "Glamorous" with the backing music from the Fray's "She Is." The result is a high-style rap video against a piano-based musical composition. It has been viewed nearly 200,000 times at YouTube and is widely posted across dozens of other sites.

Another recent form of mashup is using trailer clips from movies and combining them to make "new" movie trailers. (Trailers introduce the public to an upcoming movie.) Mashups also occur in film. The movie *Forrest Gump* has several scenes where historical footage is combined with scenes of Tom Hanks's character. The original dialogue is replaced so that it seems like Hanks's character was there.

 Historical figures and modern-day actors can meet on the screen. Clips such as this one combine historical footage of John F. Kennedy with actor Tom Hanks.

Another form of video mashup is a combination of unrelated clips and/or sound tracks. This has been done for years in television. Comedy shows use real video footage of famous people and events but remove the original sound track. They replace the sound track with new lines of dialogue (words) or music. The mashup is usually a parody of what that person sounds like.

 Visit www.thetrailermash.com to view amazing mashups, such as *Titanic: Two the Surface* by Robert Blankenheim. He combined clips from more than twenty trailers and films to make a fake sequel to the movie *Titanic*. Leonardo DiCaprio's character is brought back to life

Web sites like TheTrailerMash (www.thetrailermash.com) share examples of how creative you can get with video trailer footage, vocal tracks, and sound tracks.

after being frozen on the ocean's floor (http://www. thetrailermash.com/titanic-two-the-surface-sequel).

Software Mashups

You can combine elements of software to make a new application. This mashup has developed over the last few years. Software is made with thousands of lines of code. Code tells the computer what to do. People who write the code are programmers. Programmers and non-programmers can produce software mashups using various tools. Certain companies, such as Google, Yahoo!, and eBay make their data available to the public. Their sites have special linking programs, called application programming interfaces, or API, that allow you to "take" portions of their content and reuse them in your own application or Web site.

You can pull content from Google and mix it with content from the site Craigslist. Merging content from Google and Craigslist was done—to great success—by Paul Rademacher in 2005. He was frustrated by the process of hunting for a place to live. He could not see all the listings on one map. He created HousingMaps (www. housingmaps.com), which blends the map feature from Google with the housing listings from Craigslist. You're able to see all the listings on one map with links to each listing on the right. According to *BusinessWeek*, more than half a million people viewed his Web site within the first three months. Google was so impressed with Paul's work that it hired him. Using the Google and other online map features is now called mapping. According to CNET Networks, about ten new mapping mashups are made each day.

CHAPTER TWO

SHOWCASING AN INDIVIDUAL VISION

We can escape from the real world around us into the virtual world of the Web. Software mashups, however, are bringing the world around us back to us. What is happening in your neighborhood? More specifically, what's happening on your street? Is your street safe? Are there times that are safer to be on it than others? What is the history of your street, as far as crime goes? Do you live in a neighborhood that is in need of a Neighborhood Watch program? You could type a few keywords into a search engine like Google or Yahoo! to find out, but you would get a lot of links that you would have to review individually. What if there were a Web site that would tell you this information, all at once?

A mashup of two Web sites, maps.google.com and www.chicagocrime.com, shows a neighborhood in Chicago where a crime—motor vehicle theft—was committed.

Adrian Holovaty, who has a background in journalism, made a mashup site that does just that. He thought it would be helpful to see what sort of crimes were occurring on a neighborhood basis. It could allow a person to be more comfortable on his or her streets. It could also allow someone to consider doing something, such as starting a Neighborhood Watch, in high-crime areas. The Web site is www.chicagocrime.org. It merges mapping from Google and crime reports from the Chicago Police Department's Citizen ICAM site. His site covers crimes that have been reported throughout the Chicago area. You can enter a specific address, and a list of crimes will display with a map.

You can also search nearby crimes by two, four, and eight blocks. When you click on the individual crime, it shows detailed information, such as whether an arrest was made and the exact location and time of the crime. According to *BusinessWeek*, within the first few weeks of its creation, the site attracted 1.2 million surfers. This demonstrated that people would consider using a mashup to learn about their safety.

An Idea Leads to a Whole New Future

Holovaty mixed his love for journalism with online news sites, and it proved profitable. He spends his time thinking about how to make online news sites more helpful to us in general. There is a wealth of information that can be mashed to make our lives better. Holovaty was awarded a $1.1 million grant in 2007 for wanting to do just that. The grant comes from the John S. and James L. Knight Foundation. His goal is to "create an

MUSIC, VIDEO, AND SOFTWARE MASHUPS

 A simple idea about an ideal Web site that doesn't yet exist can lead to big things. Pictured here is Adrian Holovaty, creator of www.chicagocrime.org.

easy way to answer the question, 'What is happening around me?'" He will be quitting his job as the editor of Editorial Innovations at washingtonpost.com to make his goal happen. He will be founding a Web startup company called EveryBlock and will hire a team of Web developers to make the most out of the content of online news sites.

CHECK IT OUT Check out Holovaty's crime site, as well as his other projects, such as Django. Django is a Web site where you can learn about making software mashups. He offers tools and advice. His project Web page is: http://www. holovaty.com/content/projects.

Supportive Community, Support Your Creativity

Some organizations are fully supportive of maximizing all there is to offer on their Web sites. Paul Levine, general manager of Yahoo! Local told *BusinessWeek* that community participation is essential. It allows companies like Yahoo! to learn what they need to do better and what is really needed by Web surfers. By seeing—and offering—what the public wants, they are able to keep ahead of their competitors.

Mashup technology is so new that these organizations have not yet built business models on the service. A business model allows a company to understand the service's future and the profit it will bring. The companies may eventually charge a fee for letting mashers use their data, but for now it is free. You may just want to take advantage of these supportive offerings while you still can.

You're only limited by your imagination. Most tools and applications that could help you are found online. There are also demo versions of applications across music, video, and software, which are free for a limited time. ("Demo" is short for "demonstration.") You may be able to create your masterpiece for free, before the software demo expires. Not having to worry about expensive software and editing tools can free up your creativity.

Ask yourself a few organizational questions about your project and do a bit of online research to find the answers:

- What is my goal in creation of this mashup?
- Has this already been done by someone else?
- If it's been done, how will mine be different?
- What are people saying about projects that are similar?
- Who is my audience?
- What tools seem easiest to use in order to accomplish this?
- Are there free tools that will help me with this particular project?

MUSIC, VIDEO, AND SOFTWARE MASHUPS

Major artists like David Bowie are recognizing the Web and mashups as a great way to reach and celebrate their fans. Here, Bowie receives the 2007 Webby Lifetime Achievement Award.

Seeing Things Come to Life

Just as organizations respond to great software mashups, musicians and artists respond to music and video mashups. Singer Kylie Minogue was featured in a mashup in 2002. It combined her song "Can't Get You Out of My Head" with "Blue Monday" from the band New Order. The result is "Can't Get Blue Monday Out of My Head," which is a dynamic mashup of her vocal track over New Order's techno-style beats. Minogue actually loved the version and asked Erol Alkan (then known as Kurtis Rush) to make a version for her own use. She released it on the b-side of her single "Love at First Sight." She even performed it—with New Order's backing music—at the Brit Awards in 2002.

Opportunities abound for budding mashup artists. David Bowie is another artist who supports mashups. He holds contests, which started in 2004, where he allows full use of his music for mashup artists. His contest site links to ACIDplanet.com, where you can download a variety of editing software for free. ACIDplanet has several remix contests, with prizes ranging from high-end automobiles and cash to a chance to become a guest sound engineer for a major artist. They allow you to use the music, but usage—or how something is to be used—has limitations. Contestants cannot use the mashups on other sites, only on theirs.

Copyright and Ownership

Nearly all works of art belong to their creators. In the case of musicians, the works may also belong to the record label that represents them. Video and films may also have shared owners. A copyright gives an artist the exclusive right to publish and distribute his or her work. It also prevents others from copying and selling the work. If others are caught violating a person's copyright, that person can sue. Therefore, copyright is designed to protect an artist's work.

Most artists have signed lengthy contracts with their record labels, management teams, and album distributors. Every detail is considered, and every revenue stream is analyzed and divided. A revenue stream is a line of income that comes from the sale of something. Music, videos, and related merchandise can be sold on the Web, on cable television, and in retail stores. All three of these represent a stream of income that must be managed. When you download your favorite music, you're paying your favorite artist's income as well as his or her support team.

Mashups bring a complicated layer to the income issue. Many song and video files can be obtained on the Internet for free because fans, as well as hackers, post them. Most mashups are free because they are considered bootlegs. A bootleg is an illegal copy of something. While an artist like David Bowie may be all right with having his music used in mashups, others are not.

WATCH OUT Since most creative works are owned by someone, be aware of the copyright laws regarding the sources you use for your mashups. Never try to sell copyrighted materials. There are several artists who support mashups so long as you do not try to make a profit off of your work. Safe mashing is better than illegal mashing!

Cease-and-Desist: Stop What You're Doing, in the Name of the Law!

Party Ben, otherwise known as Ben Gill, created a track-by-track mashup of Green Day's *American Idiot* album. Party Ben's mashup "Boulevard of Broken Songs" is one of the most well-known mashups to date. It combines Green Day's "Boulevard of Broken Dreams," Oasis's "Wonderwall," and "Writing to Reach You" by Travis. It also has Aerosmith's "Dream On" sampled from Eminem's "Sing for the Moment." It became an instant hit among mashup fans.

Mashup artists use the Web as a way to showcase and share their works. Pictured here is Party Ben's site, www.partyben.com, where you can download his mashups and latest projects.

Ben's site was up for only ten days. Green Day's record label, Warner Music, e-mailed Party Ben, ordering him to close the site. He did so, but not without the public noticing. A fellow mashup artist named Noisehead launched AmericanEdit.org, where he instructed the community to protest Warner Music's actions.

AmericanEdit.org's protest was modeled off of another famous mashup protest in 2004. A DJ named Danger Mouse produced *The Grey Album*. It was a mashup of the Beatles' music from *The White Album* and Jay-Z's rapping and lyrics from his *Black Album*. EMI—the owners of the Beatles' music—served DJ Danger Mouse with a cease-and-desist order. This is a

MUSIC, VIDEO, AND SOFTWARE MASHUPS

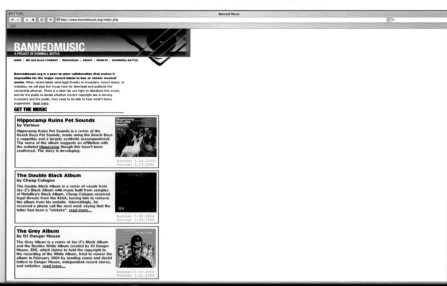

Major-label control over music is seen by some artists as a great annoyance. It limits creativity. Artists like Jay-Z and Linkin Park worked with their labels to produce mashups, which were posted on www.bannedmusic.org.

legal order to stop all action and remove a project from public space.

The original protest occurred on February 24, 2004. It was called Grey Tuesday. A group called Downhill Battle put the request out over the Web that fans post the album on their sites for free downloading. They also asked supporters to turn their Web site pages grey for the day. According to MTV, just under 200 sites posted the album, and it was downloaded more than 100,000 times. About 250 Web sites went grey. This showed the record label community that there are savvy consumers out there, but how to approach copyright issues is a difficult subject.

The new protest for Party Ben's mashup album was equally noticed by fans. Even though both projects are deemed illegal because of copyright issues, you can find audio and video of the works online. Sites such as YouTube have search features where you can key in the title of these bootleg mashups, and you'll find some version, if not the original.

The response of the online community on Grey Tuesday is an indication of the power of the Web. It is a great medium for getting messages distributed, as well as mashups. A medium is a means for communication. *Entertainment Weekly* named *The Grey Album* the 2004 Record of the Year. Jay-Z actually supports remixing and offers a vocal track already isolated for the purposes of mashing. His record label, Roc-A-Fella, took no legal action against Danger Mouse for *The Grey Album*. Later in 2004, Jay-Z and Linkin Park created *MTV Ultimate Mash-Ups Presents Jay-Z/Linkin Park: Collision Course*.

CHAPTER THREE

A MIXED MEDIA COLLAGE

What form of mashup appeals to you most? For each form, there are hundreds of resources on the Web. There are hundreds of clubs and forums to join. By joining, you'll engage with a larger community of mashers. They range in expertise from newbie to seasoned professional. In online communities you can pick up tips and links to tools that others like to use. You can reduce the time it takes to learn about your kind of mashup because you're learning from other people's successes and failures. You also will be able to see how media is being used in new and interesting ways.

There are hundreds of online contests. Contests are a great way to get into mashups. This is because each

Major companies like Sony (www.acidplanet.com) use the Web to allow music fans to try their skills at mashups and other video and sound projects.

sponsor site will have a detailed description of what they expect. They will tell you the format or file type that you need to send data as. They will tell you how long it should be, and what sort of content it should include. Many sites will offer free versions of editing software that you can use for the contest. After the contest is over, you can continue using the software if you like it.

Software development companies like Sony Creative Software try to engage the mashup community with Web sites like ACIDplanet. They hold dozens of contests for music and video mashups and remixes. It is free to submit and free to register as a member. Prizes include professional suites of video- and music-editing software. Winning also introduces you as a wizard to the mashup community. The company offers free application downloads, including ACID XPress, which is a ten-track mixing and composing application for music. The video editor Vegas Movie Studio is also available. Contestants do not have to use this software to participate.

QUICK TIP Try to start your career without spending too much money on software. Simple versions of music and video editors can be found online, along with manuals and support forums. Trying demo versions is also a great way to find out what applications fit best for your uses.

Your Work in Front of Giants!

Another great thing about contests is the judges. Many judges are famous industry people who most of us will never get the chance to meet. The Sunlight Foundation

A successful mashup or idea can lead to Web services that do not exist yet. Pictured here is Craig Newmark, creator of Craigslist (www.craigslist.com), which brings the global community closer together.

holds contests for the best politically based software mashups. The foundation focuses on making information about politicians more accessible. If a politician believes in a certain cause, it is good to know if this interest is motivated because of contributions or an actual concern for voters.

The foundation challenges mashers to make mashups that help us understand our politicians better. The judges for these contests are extremely impressive. They have included Esther Dyson, Craig Newmark, and Jimmy Wales. Ester Dyson is a well-known tech expert who has helped companies like Flickr get off the ground. Craig Newmark is the creator of Craigslist. Jimmy Wales is the founder of Wikipedia. Imagine these industry giants

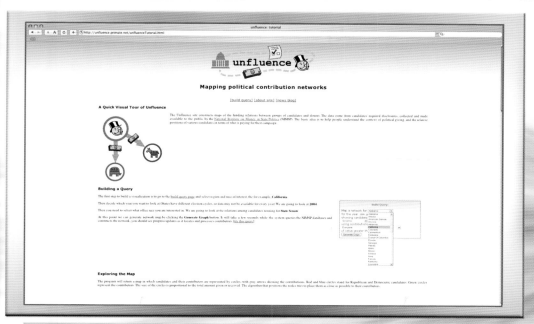

 Mashups are a great way to take complicated ideas and make them user-friendly. This mashup, unfluence.primate.net, explains what government officials are collecting in funds and from whom, which can influence legislation.

using your mashup and thinking "Wow, that's a clever way to use the Web!"

The winners of Sunlight's Mashup Congress and Win Contest created a mashup that tells us just who is giving what to each politician. Skye Bender-deMoll and Greg Michalec created Unfluence. It is a mashup that creates a map of state contributions to politicians. It merges information from the National Institute on Money in State Politics (NIMSP) and Project Vote Smart. You enter a query about the state and office (governor, Senate, House of Representatives). You select a lobby group from which contributions might come (everyone, anti-gun control, the media) and the dollar amount. The program generates a chart of politicians and their contributors.

Take a look at other mashups that are politically based. Can you take some of these mashup ideas and apply them to what else interests you? See www. sunlightfoundation.com/mashup.

At Home and School

If you don't have a computer at home, try your school library or digital lab. Tell your librarian what you would like to do. Ask if there is already software installed on the computers for editing. If there isn't, ask if the free software applications can be installed so that you may create your mashups. Software that is free is often called freeware or shareware.

Music

When dealing with music, there are several elements that you can modify. They include the speed of the song, or the tempo, and the pitch, which is the note. You can add effects with the right software, such as echoes and delay. When dealing with two tracks, you will need to match the beats of one to the other. This is called beatmatching. There are several music-editing software programs available. Some have beatmatching and others do not. For those that do not, you can use additional programs like Tap Tempo and MixMeister. Free software includes ACID XPress, Reaper, Pro Tools FREE, and Audacity.

There is additional software that enhances your DJ library, such as Rapid Evolution. This program allows you to save information about each song, as well as any comments or notes that you need to keep track of, such as the beats per minute (BPM). Other programs for purchase are MixCraft, MixMeister, Sony ACID Pro, Ableton Live, Sound Forge, Peak, and Audition. Some players also allow a video track so that you could sync or bring together your music mashup with a video. An example is WaveLab.

You must render or translate the audio file into a format that players will be able to read. These sound files include MP3/MP4 and WAV formats. Players such as QuickTime, Windows Media Player, and RealPlay are common players. You will also want to think about where your final project will end up being displayed. If it is for a contest, follow the rules about the type of format to submit. If it's for a community site like Yahoo!, Google, or YouTube, follow their requirements.

Video

Video has many elements that you can modify. You will be determining when a clip will begin and end. You will decide what clips go where to make a sequence of scenes. You may decide to loop video or rerun a sequence. Most operating systems come with simple video editors, such as iMovie for Mac and Windows Movie Maker. Other free editors include VirtualDub, WAS, Avedit, Virtual Edit, and Avid Free DV. Editors priced under $100 include Roxio Easy Media Creator, Vegas Movie Studio Plus DVD, Magix Movie Edit Pro, Pinnacle Studio Plus, Premiere Elements, and Ulead Video Studio.

Some editing tools make it easy to upload to specific sites. With the click of your mouse, CyberLink Power

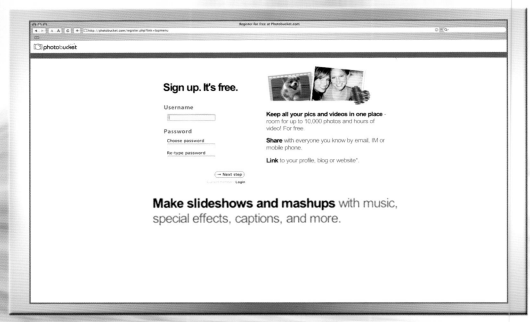

 You can find several organizations that offer free tools and services for your mashup ideas. Shown here is the Photobucket Web site (http://photobucket.com), which promotes its free mashup tools.

Director sends your finished mashup straight to YouTube. Companies like Photobucket have produced free online video editing applications so that you can house and edit video and clips while at the site. Photobucket allows for audio to be uploaded, as well as Eyespot, JumpCut, and Yahoo! Video Tool. By using Cuts, you can access and use videos from YouTube, Google, and MySpace for your mashup.

WATCH OUT When downloading software, make sure it comes from a reliable source. Downloads can contain viruses and worms. Make sure you read the system requirements as well. If you do not have some of the elements, the application won't work, and you may have to spend unnecessary money to use it.

Software

Creating a software mashup commonly involves programming. If you don't know code, you can use applications that will do the work for you. A popular free browser is Mozilla's Firefox. Greasemonkey is an extension that you add to Firefox. It allows you to add scripts to your browsing experience where you can change the look, feel, and navigation of a Web site. It is essentially creating a mashup of your favorite site. There are hundreds of scripts that are already made; all you have to do is download them from the Greasemonkey script library. The program "remembers" your mods so each time you visit that site, your new modification is there. A popular script is YouTube Googler. This script takes YouTube videos and displays them as they are displayed on Google Video, where videos fill a large portion of your monitor. If you use Safari, you can use Creammonkey for Web mashups.

In addition to using Greasemonkey, you can try other online software mashup applications like Yahoo!'s Pipes (http://pipes.yahoo.com/pipes). You use the site to build your mashups. This site offers tutorials, as well as a daily list of "Hot Pipes." Hot Pipes are user-submitted mashups that you can view and try while within the Yahoo! Pipes Web site. This can also give you ideas when trying to consider what content to mash. Developers from IBM and other major organizations give tutorials on the site.

Web sites like Pipes (http://pipes.yahoo.com/pipes) do all the hard work for you, stepping you through combining features of various sites to make your own mashup.

TECH TOOLS If you have never programmed before, start with Web application mashups. The Greasemonkey site is http://www.greasespot.net. Scripts is: http://userscripts.org. Greasemonkey makes many resources available so that when you're ready to write your own script, you'll have support. Free programming manual: http://diveintogreasemonkey.org.

Software companies are just now beginning to produce stand-alone applications for mashing. Kapow Technologies offers OpenKapow, which allows novice mashers to mash content from almost any Web site. This service walks you through building a virtual robot for

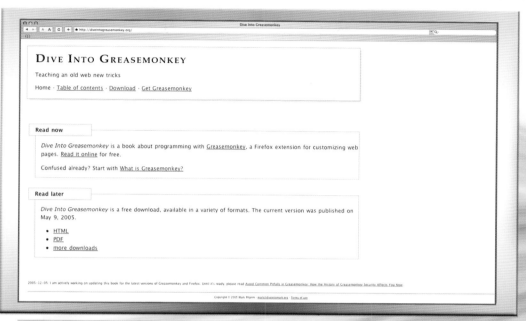

Dive Into Greasemonkey (http://diveintogreasemonkey.org) is a book and tutorial on how to use Greasemonkey to produce Web mashups. The book can be read online for free.

each site you want to access. The robot is a data collector that goes to the site and collects the information that is desired for a mashup. It continues through steps until the desired mashup is produced.

There are a few applications that allow someone without coding experience to build mapping mashups. Examples are MapBuilder and Wayfaring. Using these applications allows you to bring mapping to your site with a minimal of coding or no coding whatsoever.

Several organizations or companies have API sites, where they instruct you on how to access and use their content for your mashup purposes. Most of these services are free or can direct you to free services related to their

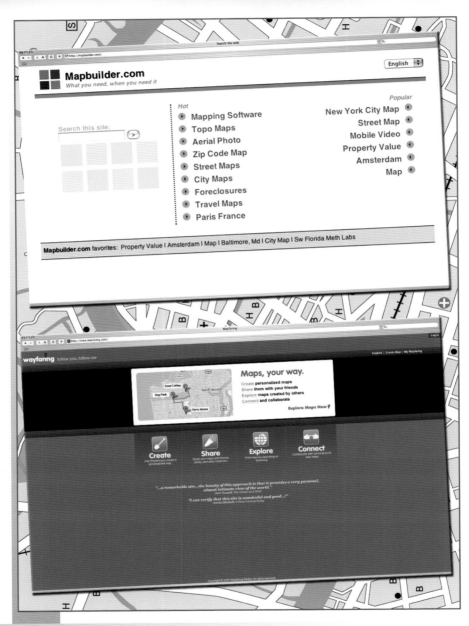

Sites like MapBuilder.com allow you to make a Google and Yahoo! map for your own purposes. These maps can be used for hundreds of interesting projects.

Web's features. They may ask that you sign up, providing a user name and a password, in order to access their tutorials or content.

In addition to Google, Yahoo!, and eBay, there is Microsoft's Start.com, Microsoft Virtual Earth, YouTube (with tutorials to help novice mashers), Flickr, Amazon, and CNET. One of the largest Web sites for software mashups is Programmable Web (www. programmableweb.com). This site will guide you to the tools you will need to do your specific mashup idea. There is also an extensive list of mashups, ranging from fun and entertaining to socially conscious applications designed to better our lives.

CHAPTER FOUR

BUILDING YOUR CREATIVE SKILLS

Mashup creators are people who see the world in a different way. What is before them is interesting, but how can it be made better? Reviews on music and video mashup sites commonly state that a mashup version is even cooler than the original projects. Mashers think of ways to offer a different view of something that is probably already pretty good. These artists are interested in voicing their opinions through mashups. Some have something funny to say and others have something serious to express. Mashups are a fun and engaging way to put your communication skills to the test.

A core skill for mashups is creativity. Some see creativity as inborn, but it can actually be developed.

A masher views his new software Web mashup on two different computer platform versions to see how it looks.

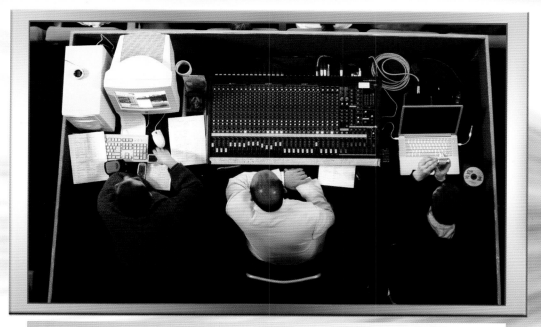

An assistant, a sound engineer, and a director work in a digital recording studio to produce a record.

Challenge your creativity by thinking critically about mashups and other art projects. Why does this mashup work? Why were these sources used to make it? How was it made and how could it be made better? What is the masher trying to communicate with this work? These questions, applied to many things, help engage and build your creativity.

The mashup community is made up of all levels of creative people. Many have jobs within the fields of the mashups they make. This is because once you know a great deal about a field, you can draw on that knowledge—and the tools you already have—to have fun. Sound engineers make mashups in their spare time. Graphic artists manipulate visual images and video in clever ways. Computer programmers and software developers get into the coolest technologies but use downtime to try to make that technology even cooler. Sometimes mashups have nothing to do with the careers of their creators, such as teacher, nurse, or student hobbyist.

QUICK TIP When you show your work for the first time to the online community, try not to worry too much about negative comments and feedback. Most successful mashers chuckle at their own junior attempts and take any criticism in stride.

As many tools are free, and most public libraries offer computer use, money is not necessarily a limiting factor in your development as a masher. One major skill that can free up many other limitations is having a working ease with computers and applications. There are detailed manuals on operating systems and applications. Take the time to read them.

Go online and research what users think of platforms and applications for specific uses. Find out how some of your favorite mashups were made. Is there a demo available for that tool? Orient yourself toward an ease in computer use. You can take classes or online tutorials.

Most software applications come with electronic versions of the manual and demonstrations. Take time to school yourself in these tutorials. You'll learn neat tricks and gain a professional ease with the application.

 Your school may have a cool outlet for your mashup skills. Here, a student works at her high school radio station as a DJ and announcer.

Making Music Part of Your Day and Pay

You will need to develop a good ear for sound. You can do this by thinking analytically, or analyzing what you hear when you listen to music. You can train your ear to pick up on certain sounds. Have you heard that sound before? What effects are added to that sound? You will also be training your memory. Soon you'll remember which songs have which effects, and how they could be used somewhere else.

It is helpful to know about musical notes and keys so that you'll be able to understand why some things sound great together and others do not. You will also discover that some things that sound bad together somehow still work as a composition. Some instruments will actually cancel each other out if improperly mixed or recorded. These are the dynamics of sound. You can learn about the principles of sound dynamics in music classes, audio engineering school, and online tutorials. Having a background in sound dynamics will make your mashups more polished.

You don't need to know how to play an instrument to be a sound engineer. You don't need to know how to sing to be a producer. You do need an enthusiasm for the art form as well as a desire to create. Other roles that can supplement a budding music mashup career are DJ, musical artist, and music critic.

Communicating Through Visual Images

Video is a visual medium. The lighting, scenery, plotting of characters/objects, and action of a work are all elements

Career Questions

Answer a few of the following questions if you're considering a career in music, video, or computer technology. If you find your answer is yes to more than a few, you may have found a short- or long-term career goal.

DJ—Do you love sharing your music with others? Do you know a lot of little-known facts about a type of music? Do you search out various versions of a song you love?

Sound Engineer—Does the world of sound fascinate you? Do you manip- ulate your stereo's features to make your favorite music sound better? Do you have a home studio set up already?

Music Producer—When you hear a song, do you think about how it could be better? Does just listening to music give you ideas about other songs? Do you analyze what makes a work better than others?

Graphic Artist/Animator—Do you love to paint, draw, or take photos? Do you make projects for friends and family? Is art the easiest way for you to express yourself?

Director—Do you love watching and analyzing great films? Have you already made a video project? Does the idea of bringing a script to life excite you?

Web Designer—Do you spend hours surfing the Web? Do you analyze what features on Web sites you like to use and which you don't? Are you curious about how they work and how the Web works?

Programmer—Do you already know how to read the source code on a Web browser when you click "view source"? Do you have a natural desire to solve detailed challenges? Are you comfortable with mathematical equations?

Developer—Do computers, and what they can do, fascinate you? Do you compare applications to each other and analyze the differences? Do you think of ways that applications can better serve your needs?

that engage the eyes. They are also ways to communicate ideas and messages to others. Dark, moody lighting makes a person feel scared or depressed. Bright light is translated as cheerful. These are the elements of film.

Seeking a career in film can supplement your goals in video mashup and allow you access to high-end tools. There are individuals in film that do not have film degrees, but many do. This is so they can advance quickly in the industry. Studying film will give you a broad skill set so that you may choose from a variety of roles. You study the history of film, equipment, and techniques. You could be a producer, screenwriter, camera operator, director, or actor. To be successful in roles within the film industry, you need to understand how the moving image tells a story.

Art

Graphic design is another visual field that lends itself well to mashups. In studying graphic design, you learn about shape, color, illustration, photography, and using the computer to produce art. This includes using applications like Macromedia Director to produce short-length films.

Some mashers include custom-designed images in their work. Being able to add custom images to make mashups more interesting is a skill. You'll want to make them blend in with the images that are there. Applications allow you to make title pages and credits, but with graphic design skills you could build an animated intro of your title, your name, or your production company's name. This adds to the overall professional look of your projects.

 Students sit at computer stations where they are learning to use Mac-based design programs.

Making an Application Even Better

If you have ever added an extension or plug-in to your favorite application, you've already done some custom scripting without knowing it. You changed the out-of-the-box form of your program by adding new code. While you didn't write the code, you're getting there. You're beginning to think like a programmer and developer. Having a career as either will help build your mashup skills, especially if you love software mashups. You will be able to modify your software mashup or the applications that help you build software mashups.

CHAPTER FIVE

MASHUPS FOR PROFIT AND NONPROFIT USES

When you read comments about popular music and video mashups, you will find a repeating theme. People change their minds about how they felt about the sources used in the work. For DJ Lobsterdust's "She Is Glamorous," you can see an evenly spread slate of comments stating that a person didn't like the artists Fergie or the Fray until watching and listening to the mashup. Many recording and video artists secretly support mashups for this very reason. It is promotion for their career, even if they are not making any money off of it directly.

Most music mashers do not make money off of their work as the content does not belong to them. There are a

Music mashers, such as DJ Lobsterdust (www.djlobsterdust.com), use the Web to showcase their work. Online exposure can often lead to real-life gigs.

few mashers who have produced legal versions of works and are making a profit. Mark Vidler is a well-known and genuinely accomplished music masher. He is also the first masher to work with a major record label to release the first legally cleared mashup album. It is called *Mashed*. Vidler, who manages Go Home Productions, worked with EMI to clear the rights to use works from artists such as the Doors, Blondie, Madonna, No Doubt, Malcolm McLaren, and Iggy Pop. Two other mashers, Loo and Placido, contributed to the album as well.

A CLOSER LOOK You can listen to samples of all of the *Mashed* works at Go Home Production's Web site: http://www.gohomeproductions. co.uk/mashed/home.html.

No. 1 on the Charts

Mark Vidler's "Rapture Riders," a mashup of the bands Blondie and the Doors, came onto the Billboard charts at number 1. The voice of Jim Morrison, lead singer of the Doors, haunts the echoing rock of Blondie's backing music. The remix was featured on Blondie's greatest hits collection. Vidler's skill in mashing has allowed him to work as a remixer for huge talents like Alicia Keys, David Bowie, and Gang of Four. Vidler is an example of someone who has turned a love for mashups into a profitable, globally recognized venture. Because the art form is so new and wide open, anyone can be the next Mark Vidler.

If you're planning a long-term career in mashups, do everything you can to know all about the type you like. Join forums and take part in community discussions.

 Mashed (www.gohomeproductions.co.uk/mashed) is described as the "ultimate bootleg album," but it is actually a legally cleared mashup of several major-label recording artists such as Madonna, No Doubt, Kelis, and Iggy Pop.

Analyze the field and what people seem to respond to the most. The community of mashup fans isn't made up entirely of mashers. They are YouTubers and music and film buffs as well. Whether you're making a video parody of a U.S. president or making an homage, or tribute, to your favorite band, there is an audience eager to receive it.

At some point in the future, there will be a viable way for you to sell your projects to this audience. Are there any mashups in your desired form that are being sold currently? What sort of products are these and who is buying them? Learning about business practices ahead of time will help you when mashups get to the for-purchase level. Explore your local resources, such as colleges that offer summer courses. Take classes in the business of the arts so that you can learn all there is to know about legal practices and making profits in the arts.

TECH TOOLS You can use *Wired* magazine's *The Wired CD* to create legal mashups. *Wired* magazine cleared the rights with several well-known artists to allow you to "Rip. Sample. Mash. Share." See http://creativecommons.org/wired (no www). Artists include the Beastie Boys, Le Tigre, Chuck D, and David Byrne (from Talking Heads).

Making a Go of Mashups

The creator of Greasemonkey is Aaron Boodman. He is a Web developer for Google. Programmers and developers in full-time jobs can afford to provide new and interesting services like Greasemonkey for free. In the future, features like this may come with fees, but for now, most software mashup applications are free to the public.

Boodman told *BusinessWeek* that "technology is finally growing up and making it [mashing] possible." He believes the Web was originally designed to be mashed. The Web is an inherently public space, where we go for free information. The very nature of the Web means that even as fees and profits start coming into play, free mashup tools will still be available.

You may design something, legally cleared, that truly serves the public. It will be up to you if you want to charge a fee for it or make a profit off of it. Oftentimes, if you make something truly valuable, companies with the same goal will contact you. They may offer to buy or license your project, or hire you, as in the case of

 The Beastie Boys are like several other artists who want to make their work available on sites like www.creativecommons.org to innovative people such as mashers and producers, without high license fees.

HousingMaps's creator, Paul Rademacher. Rademacher was a software engineer at DreamWorks Animation before getting Google's attention.

Making It Legal

Creative Commons, where you can obtain *The Wired CD*, is a nonprofit organization. Its motto is, "Share, reuse, and remix—legally." Its goal is to make tools and content legally accessible and also free. Authors, educators, scientists, and artists visit the site to change and list their copyright conditions. This allows you to search through the database to find content that you like.

Each work will have usage issues clearly defined. Keywords are "attribution," "noncommercial," "no derivatives," and "share alike." "Attribution" means you must name where your content comes from. "Noncommercial" means that you can use the work, but not for a profit. "No derivatives" means you may use the work as is and cannot edit it. "Share alike" means you can use the materials, but only if your finished project is also posted in Creative Commons under the same terms.

The Free Software Foundation offers a similar service as Creative Commons, but for software programming and development. Users can copy, modify, use, and redistribute any of the programs and scripts in the database. If you love a certain feature of the Web or an application, but don't have a clue how it's coded, this is the place to start. You can openly access the script of similar features to study how the code was written. Then you can copy and paste it into your work!

 Because mashups are able to bring attention to artists, works of art, Web services, Web sites, and great causes, many tools such as ww.fsf.org are available for free on the Web.

 Visit Creative Commons to find out what content you can use, legally free and clear: http://creativecommons.org. Check out free content for programming software at: http://www.fsf.org.

It's Up to You

Mashup is a form that is so truly new, there is so much room for innovation. Bring your energy and creativity to this form and give it even more momentum or speed. Computer-based technology is always changing; even programmers strive to keep up with the latest technology. Don't get discouraged if mastering a certain software

Build a Professional Profit-Making Portfolio

Mashup, whether music, video, or software, is an art that requires developing skills. Your first mashup will pale in comparison to your 100th. Your skills, by then, will showcase a seasoned editor and creative thinker. Don't stop at making just one or two great mashups. Make as many as you can. This will become your portfolio. Offering a variety of mashups to listen to, view, or use can show any potential employer how skilled and creative you are. Skilled and creative thinkers are an asset to any company.

Your work will need to be exhibited somewhere that is easily accessible. You can burn CDs and DVDs, which you can distribute, but this can be costly. A great solution is a Web site. Web services start at around $10 a month, depending on the features that you want. If you do not have Web-building skills, look for a service provider that has easy Web-building applications.

If you're housing videos and music mashups on your site, make sure that you include disclaimers about the content. Common disclaimers include "For demonstration purposes only, not for resale. Original copyright belongs to . . ." For video works, especially if there is humor, you can write "For parody purposes only." Provide an e-mail link where copyright owners can contact you if they need to.

If you wanted to fully maximize your mashup skills, the next challenge would be building a software mashup for your online portfolio. What cool features could you add? You could list the artists you use in your mashups and merge it with mapping. You could pull the Google map feature and show where each artist you featured resides. The possibilities of showing your hirable skills are endless.

application is remaining challenging. Always turn to the source: the Web. You'll be able to find several papers (called White Papers), academic Web sites, software development help pages, and individual sites. As long as your patience, dedication, and enthusiasm remain, you'll find your work alongside industry giants in no time.

GLOSSARY

a cappella Singing without using musical instruments.

bootleg An illegally reproduced copy of a form of software or media.

composition A complete artistic or literary work.

consumer A buyer of goods and services.

demo Short for demonstration; used to show features, use, or purpose.

dialogue Conversation between two or more people.

format The form in which something is produced, saved, and transferred.

freeware Software or applications that are free to use or download.

homage A tribute of respect or honor to someone or something.

isolate To put something by itself; to set apart from the others.

master A final version of a recording session.

medium A means for communication.

modify To change something from its original form.

parody To mimic or make fun of something in a similar way.

producer Someone who brings various elements together to create something.

remix A modified version of an original song.

render To translate or make something available.

revenue stream A line of income that comes from the sale of something.

sync To bring two things together so they are in time with one another.

tempo The rate or speed of a song.

track A channel of a recording system on which a sound is recorded.

trailer Clips of scenes that introduce a coming movie to the public.

usage How something is to be used or is used.

FOR MORE INFORMATION

Computer Graphics Society
Aldgate Valley Road
Mylor, SA 5153
Australia
E-mail: info@cgsociety.org
Web site: http://www.cgsociety.org
The Computer Graphics Society is a global organization for creative digital artists. CGS supports "artists at every level by offering a range of services to connect, inform, educate and promote, by celebrating achievement, excellence and innovation in all aspects of digital art."

Society of Professional Audio Recording Services (SPARS)
4300 Tenth Avenue North
Lake Worth, FL 33461
(561) 641-6648
Web site: http://www.spars.com
SPARS is an organization that provides information and programs about the music recording industry. Its services include placing interns, educational seminars, regional meetings, networking, and counseling.

Sunlight Foundation
1818 N Street NW, Suite 410
Washington, DC 20036
(202) 742-1520
E-mail: info@sunlightfoundation.com
Web site: http://www.sulightfoundation.com

This organization uses technology to help the public learn about their elected representatives. You can join forums, learn about mashups, and submit your software and Web mashups to its contests.

TechSoup.org
435 Brannan Street, Suite 100
San Francisco, CA 94107
(415) 633-9300
E-mail: info@techsoup.org
Web site: http//www.techsoup.org
TechSoup is an organization that is dedicated to making technology available to nonprofit organizations and individuals within these organizations. Its Web site's features include a learning center where anyone can learn more about new technologies like software mashups.

Web Sites

Due to the changing nature of Internet links, Rosen Publishing has developed an online list of Web sites related to the subject of this book. This site is updated regularly. Please use this link to access the list:

http://www.rosenlinks.com/dcb/mvsm

FOR FURTHER READING

Baron, Cynthia L. *Designing a Digital Portfolio.* Indianapolis, IN: New Riders, 2003.

Burd, Barry A., and S. Hayes. *Beginning Programming with Java for Dummies.* Hoboken, NJ: John Wiley & Sons, 2005.

Byrne, P. *Computer Game and Film Graphics* (Art Off the Wall). Portsmouth, NH: Heinemann, 2006.

Hopkin, Bart. *Getting a Bigger Sound: Pickups and Microphones for Your Musical Instrument.* Tucson, AZ: See Sharp Press, 2003.

Purvis, Michael, Jeffrey Sambells, and Cameron Turner. *Beginning Google Maps Applications with PHP and Ajax: From Novice to Professional.* Berkeley, CA: Apress, 2006.

Roseman, Jordan. *Audio Mashup Construction Kit* (ExtremeTech). Hoboken, NJ: John Wiley & Sons, 2006.

Schaefer, A. R., and James Henke. *Making a First Recording* (Rock Music Library). Mankato, MN: Capstone, 2003.

Shanahan, Francis. *Amazon.com Mashups.* Hoboken, NJ: Wrox Press Incorporated, 2007.

Shulman, Mark, and Hazlitt Krog. *Attack of the Killer Video Book: Tips and Tricks for Young Directors.* Toronto, ON: Annick Press, 2004.

Wang, Wallace. *Beginning Programming for Dummies.* Hoboken, NJ: John Wiley & Sons, 2006.

BIBLIOGRAPHY

Baran, Madeleine. "Copyright and Music: A History Told in MP3s." *Stay Free! Magazine.* 2002. Retrieved June 8, 2007 (http://www.illegal-art.org/audio/historic.html).

BBC (British Broadcasting Company). "History of the Remix: 1Xtra's 'Remix Kid' Seani B Uncovers the Origins of Remixing . . ." Retrieved June 8, 2007 (http://www.bbc.co.uk/1xtra/tx/documentaries/remix.shtml).

BootCampClique. Grafyte Studios. "Tools." 2006. Retrieved June 8, 2007 (http://www.bootcampclique.com).

Brooks, Nadia. "Music Makers Get Mashed Up." *The Sun.* September 26, 2006. Retrieved June 8, 2007 (http://www.thesun.co.uk/article/0,,2004580002-2006440470,00.html).

Calore, Michael. "Web Mashups Turn Citizens into Washington's Newest Watchdogs." *Wired.* May 26, 2007. Retrieved June 8, 2007 (http://www.wired.com/politics/law/news/2007/04/maplight).

Dean, Katie. "*Grey Album* Fans Protest Clampdown." *Wired.* February 24, 2004. Retrieved June 8, 2007 (http://www.wired.com/entertainment/music/news/2004/02/62372).

DigitalJournal. "Bootlegging Culture: Investigating the Musical Mash-Up Phenomenon." December 15, 2005. Retrieved June 8, 2007 (http://www.digitaljournal.com/news/?articleID = 4340).

Frere-Jones, Sasha. "1 + 1 + 1 + 1: The New Math of Mashups." *New Yorker.* January 10, 2005. Retrieved

June 8, 2007 (http://www.newyorker.com/archive/2005/01/10/050110crmu_music).

Guardian Unlimited. "It's All in the Mix." February 2, 2006. Retrieved June 8, 2007 (http://technology.guardian.co.uk/weekly/story/0,,1699502,00.html).

Hof, Robert D. "Mix, Match, and Mutate." *BusinessWeek*. July 25, 2005. Retrieved June 8, 2007 (http://www.businessweek.com/@@76IH*ocQ34AvyQMA/magazine/content/05_30/b3944108_mz063.htm).

Kehaulani Goo, Sara. "Art and Marketing All Mashed Up." *Washington Post*. August 2, 2006. Retrieved June 8, 2007 (http://www.washingtonpost.com/wp-dyn/content/article/2006/08/01/AR2006080101134.html).

Meehan, Phillip. "Boot Camp for Beginners." Painting by Numbers. 2004. Retrieved June 8, 2007 (http://www.paintingbynumbers.com/bootcamp).

Mills, Elinor. "Mapping a Revolution with 'Mashups.'" CNET. November 17, 2005. Retrieved June 8, 2007 (http://news.com.com/Mapping + a + revolution + with + mashups/2009-1025_3-5944608.html).

Open Directory & Blog for Mashups & Web 2.0 APIs. "IBM Mashup Summit." May 9, 2007. Retrieved June 8, 2007 (http://www.webmashup.com/blog/2007/05/09/ibm-mashup-summit).

Patel, Joseph. "Grey Tuesday Group Says 100,000 Downloaded Jay-Z/Beatles Mix." MTV Networks. March 5, 2004. Retrieved June 8, 2007 (http://www.mtv.com/news/articles/1485593/20040305/jay_z.jhtml).

Purvis, Michael, Jeffrey Sambells, and Cameron Turner. *Beginning Google Maps Applications with PHP and*

Ajax: From Novice to Professional. Berkeley, CA: Apress, 2006.

Remix Theory. "Remix Defined." Retrieved June 8, 2007 (http://remixtheory.net/?page_id=3).

Satterfield, Brian. "Mashups: An Easy, Free Way to Create Custom Web Apps." TechSoup. September 8, 2006. Retrieved June 8, 2007 (http://www.techsoup. org/learningcenter/webbuilding/page5788.cfm).

Sherwin, Adam. "Just Steal My Greatest Hits, Says Bowie." TimesOnline. April 26, 2004. Retrieved June 8, 2007 (http://www.timesonline.co.uk/tol/ news/uk/article844013.ece?token=null&offset=0).

Sunlight Foundation. "The Sun Is Rising on Congress 2.0." Retrieved June 8, 2007 (http://www. sunlightfoundation.com/mashup).

Terdiman, Daniel. "Mashup Artists Face the Music." *Wired*. May 4, 2004. Retrieved June 8, 2007 (http://www.wired.com/entertainment/music/ news/2004/05/63314).

VideoMashups.ca. "Mashup Essentials." 2006. Retrieved June 8, 2007 (http://www.videomashups.ca).

Wilkinson, David M. *Flickr Mashups*. Hoboken, NJ: Wrox Press Incorporated, 2007.

INDEX

About the Author

Holly Cefrey is an award-winning children's book author. She has taken classes from the Institute of Audio Research in New York, where she learned about sound engineering and the principles of recording. Through her customized degree from New York University's Gallatin School, she was able to take digital arts and computer science classes from the various colleges at NYU. She has programmed very simple routines in C++ through coursework. She utilizes applications such as Director, Photoshop, ImageReady, Fireworks, and Flash to make short films and online graphics. She designs Web sites for friends and freelance clients in her spare time.

Photo Credits